T0120723

Armored Up:

A 30-Day Writing Journey to Combat Spiritual Warfare

SHERYL WALKER

authorHOUSE®

AuthorHouse™
1663 Liberty Drive
Bloomington, IN 47403
www.authorhouse.com
Phone: 833-262-8899

Published by AuthorHouse 10/27/2020

ISBN: 978-1-6655-0454-6 (sc)
ISBN: 978-1-6655-0453-9 (e)

Library of Congress Control Number: 2020920463

Print information available on the last page.

"God will make you so uncomfortable, you
will do the very thing you fear."
-Unknown

Warfare
Swords, grenades, and bayonets:
As you get closer to God,
Closer to a healing,
The spiritual warfare will increase.
Are you armored up?

For though we walk in the flesh, we do not war according to the flesh. For the weapons of our warfare *are* not carnal but mighty in God for pulling down strongholds, casting down arguments and every high thing that exalts itself against the knowledge of God, bringing every thought into captivity to the obedience of Christ.

- 2 Corinthians 10:3-5 King James Version (NKJV)

"Put on the whole armor of God, that you may be able to stand against the wiles of the devil. For we do not wrestle against flesh and blood, but against principalities, against powers, against the rulers of the darkness of this age, against spiritual *hosts* of wickedness in the heavenly *places*. Therefore, take up the whole armor of God, that you may be able to withstand in the evil day, and having done all, to stand.

Stand therefore, having girded your waist with truth, having put on the breastplate of righteousness, and having shod your feet with the preparation of the gospel of peace; above all, taking the shield of faith with which you will be able to quench all the fiery darts of the wicked one. And take the helmet of salvation, and the sword of the Spirit, which is the word of God."

- Ephesians 6:11-17 (NKJV)

The Bible speaks of "the full armor of God." This stands for truth, righteousness, faith, salvation, God's word, and peace.

- Belt of Truth: This is the piece of armor which is the core, that which holds the rest of the armor together. It is God's word and who we are in Christ.
- Breastplate of Righteousness: This is the piece of armor that protects our hearts. This helps us to make decisions that honor God.
- Shoes of Peace: This is the piece of armor that allows us a restful peace as we proceed through life.
- Shield of Faith: This is the piece of armor that helps us to trust God at all times. We are to lock shields with other believers.
- Helmet of Salvation: This is the piece of armor that guards our minds. We have to continue to remind ourselves that we belong to Christ. This allows us to remain focused and with a rational mind.
- Sword of the Spirit: This is the piece of armor that is God's word and truth, which we can use for direction. This is the reading of the Bible. This is the spiritual approach to battle, not the human approach.

You must armor up daily in preparation for whatever comes your way.

INTRODUCTION

There is a war going on, whether or not we are aware of it. The enemy's goal is to kill, steal, and destroy. He wants your soul. He wants to prevent you from reaching your God-ordained destiny. When we study the devil's tactics long enough, we see a pattern of negativity such as rejection, mockery, being overwhelmed with various distractions, loneliness, chaos in various forms, and mistakes and delays that overwhelm us.

This increase in warfare happens when the victory, blessing, or anointing is near. The greater the assignment, the greater the attack.

We can easily end up consumed with the negative, and not reflecting on God's goodness. One of the key ways the enemy accomplishes this is by getting into your mind. He will replay the same weaknesses over and over again. When the warfare picks up, I say to myself, "What blessing is near?" or "What am I about to do for the glory of God?"

Additionally, any gift God has placed in you is often seen as a threat to the enemy. Each and every blessing becomes an opportunity for an attack. When you reconcile broken relationships, there is an attack. When you put away anger, there is an attack. He will attack you with many different things to make you weary. The burden of attacks makes you want to give up or give in. He will keep throwing hurdles in the way so that you won't actually make progress. People and their behavior will come along as distractions to stop you from being healthy in mind, body, and spirit, and prevent you from completing your kingdom work. You can't give up! Don't fall for it.

Preparing yourself for this battle may not reduce the conflict, but it does reduce the devastation. The moments I was ill prepared, I responded to the warfare personally, as if this conflict was directed at just me. I fed into the whirlwind of events, instead of being still and remembering who God was. Having a strategic response is critical.

The Bottom Line

The bottom line is that God is a "turn it around God." He will work out everything for good. Everything evil manifesting in the physical visible world is a battle being waged in the invisible spiritual world. The good news is that the enemy has already been defeated. We will be victorious. The battle has already been won. We know the end of this story. Be strong and steadfast. Submit your request to God. Armor up in scripture, prayer, fasting, and praise. Move at key moments. Fight at key moments, when God tells you to. Weather the storm. Surrender the journey to God. The greater the warfare, the greater the impact you are making on the kingdom. God will fight with us and for us. We must not take our dependency on him lightly. Ignore the distractions. We have to live our life with the intention of magnifying God while simultaneously withstanding the enemy. Don't succumb to the attacks. STAY FOCUSED. If our insight is sufficiently keen, we see the multitude of miracles that present themselves in the midst of the battle: unique opportunities, angels that come to help in various forms, delays but not denials, and victories beyond our wildest dreams even in uncertain situations. Use the battlefield as an opportunity to get stronger and wiser.

We have to be armored up for the battle. The enemy uses the offenses from our antagonist(s) and other circumstantial situations to weaken us and to erode our faith in God. Remember ALL is for good. Not some of it: all of it. What the enemy meant for harm will work out for your good. One of the primary tasks in taking on this attack therefore lies in reframing this from "what is happening to you" to "what is happening for your own good." Satan is limited to what God allows. He is a liar and deceiver. Once we become wise to his tactics, we can forever claim victory.

The Research & Process

In exploring these ideas, I reflected on my life experiences and all the seasons that felt like warfare: intense attacks, grief, pain, criticism, and confusion. I also considered my mental, emotional and physical responses to the warfare: anger, sorrow, blame, numbing out, detaching from the experience, or simply removing myself altogether. What was the best response when the burden felt like more than I could bear? My response had generational implications. If I let the enemy win, how would this impact my children and my children's children? I had to remain focused and do what was right by God. In this book, I explore these insights and revelations.

The Structure

When I thought of a structure or format that brought me to a place of understanding in the past, I recalled a 30-day writing challenge I had participated in a few years prior, during a time I felt broken and confused by the cards life had dealt me. In retrospect, those cards were a true blessing. Daily writing often serves as an enlightenment ritual for me personally and lifts me out of darkness. This led me to reflect on how I could use my season of calamity to armor up, increase my faith in God, and declare victory over the enemy. The text is focused on the armor and weaponry for the battle.

The Outcome

Going through each day, one by one, strengthened my resolve to remain steadfast in the midst of the warfare. The storms of life are still a struggle, but I know who is in control. When you are depleted and at your wits end, God will give you supernatural strength. Each battle has served as a training ground for something greater. It reaffirms my deep knowing that "no weapon formed against me shall prosper" (Isaiah 54:17). No retaliation is needed. Just wait and see the glory of God.

Ironically, during the writing of this book (2020), the globe was suffering from the COVID- 19 pandemic, and in the USA, many were angered and outraged by the extrajudicial police killings of black people. It felt like a state of war. People were getting infected and dying at astronomical rates. Just when we thought things were better, states rebounded with the virus. This felt like intense warfare. But as believers, we know that even in what appears to be silence, God is there. What was God saying to us in the midst of the battle?

GET READY

In the subsequent pages, you will be presented with daily warfare passages. This is a series of 30 reflections on spiritual warfare, giving you meditations to carry out day by day. You will also be asked to write each day. Pour your heart out onto the pages that have been provided. Read, reflect, write, and armor up. I hope that you will benefit from this 30-day journey, and that by the end you will feel fully equipped to engage in battle.

Our passage reading and reflection plan for the next 30 days will strengthen us for the battle.

The Weaponry/Armor:

Day 1: Your Battle Plan
Day 2: Why Am I in This Battle?
Day 3: Prayer and Fasting
Day 4: Scripture and Biblical Examples
Day 5: Praise and Worship
Day 6: Follow the Prompting of the Holy Spirit and Obey
Day 7: Forgiveness
Day 8: Tithes and Offerings
Day 9: Remember God's Promises and Your Authority
Day 10: Monitor Pride
Day 11: Connect with Other Believers
Day 12: Monitor What Is Feeding Your Spirit
Day 13: Love the People in Front of You

Be sober, be vigilant; because your adversary the devil walks about like a roaring lion, seeking whom he may devour.

- 1 Peter 5:8 (NKJV)

DAY 1

Your Battle Plan

During the gravest attacks I endured, there were key things I did:

1) I let God be God.
2) I paused. Remained still, moved toward peace and quiet, prayed, and asked God for direction after each attack. I was on full alert. Structures were in place.
3) I didn't take no for an answer. I pushed when God told me to push. I followed the prompting of the Holy Spirit. I asked him explicitly, "Lord, please show me signs of when to move." And then I moved!
4) I prayed some more, fasted, and solicited other prayer warriors.
5) I asked God for strength and I asked God for rest.
6) I remained focused, present and supportive. I was extra careful, as I knew the devil would slip into any opening or any area of my life I had left unmanned. I took minimal chances.
7) I did not waver with my faith.
8) I only brought those around me that would support and add to my peace. I forgave others and worked on at least temporarily removing those that added to the chaos.
9) I didn't allow the negative to be the lasting narrative of the situation. I saw the beautiful moments God showed his face in the circumstance.
10) I read the Bible.

11) I meditated on hymns and praise music.

12) I tried not to be combative or defensive but used key windows of time to voice serious concerns.

13) I asked for help. I accepted help. I tried not to be stubborn or resistant.

14) I was quick not to judge or criticize, but to accept others, forgive, and restore.

15) I was careful with my scheduling, making sure to give myself time to recover from things that had the potential to deplete me, before taking on the next challenge.

16) I was alert to the multiple varying attacks, like a ninja. I kept my eyes open.

17) I didn't give up or give in.

18) I looked inward to see my deficiencies and what I needed to work on. What needed healing? I didn't want to operate out of my wounds. There would be dire consequences.

19) I avoided the devil.

20) I saw the beauty in the smallest things.

21) I kept my eyes fixed on my responsibilities. The devil wanted me to throw in the towel.

22) I didn't waste my energy on low-level battles. I took the feedback, but didn't waste too much energy.

23) I consistently paid my tithe and offering.

24) I exercised extra discipline in certain areas in my life such as my finances.

25) When people were mean and unfair, I did not stoop to their level.

26) I was alert to the division and isolation in the atmosphere.

There are some things you can take as given. He will attack your home, family, marriage, health, job, identity, closest relationships, and any sense of security. How will you fight back? Now your attention is on the thing and not God. The enemy will use everyone closest to you—and I mean everyone. Don't lose focus. Take care of yourself or else you won't be able to fight. The enemy will certainly wear you down—attack after attack, causing you to want to give up. Don't let him win!

Prompt 1: Before we delve into strategies to fight against warfare, I want you to consider what you are doing now as it pertains to the fight. What is your current battle plan?

_____

_____

_____

_____

_____

_____

_____

_____

_____

_____

_____

_____

_____

_____

_____

_____

_____

_____

_____

_____

_____

_____

_____

"The thief comes only to steal and kill and destroy; **I have come that they may have life**, and have it to the full."

- John 10:10 (NIV)

DAY 2

Why Am I in This Battle?

Have you ever been hit with a season of intense pressure and misfortune? There might be frequent attacks and criticism, and what appears to be people stirred up and led by demonic forces. Nothing seems to be going your way. You focus on your deficiencies, missteps, and mistakes. Fear keeps you frozen. While setbacks and calamities are part of the human experience, a spiritual attack or warfare is a different beast. The intensity is greatly heightened, as if you are drowning under pressure and despair.

Why is this happening? There is a dark force that exists—evil rulers and authorities of the unseen world. It is a force that extends beyond the person or circumstance in question. You are simply an expedient opportunity. The enemy is using these means to carry out his trickery.

This battle and warfare in the unseen realm is evident in our relationships, which become filled with division, conflict, anxieties, and overall fatigue. We find ourselves walking around with anger, fear, jealousy, and resentment, and pointing our finger at people and circumstances when we should be pointing at the unseen realm.

This is a conflict that stems from way before our time with Satan and God. Lucifer was once an angel in heaven. He rebelled against God and continues to want to undermine his authority. He is a skilled deceiver and liar, who will blind and distract us. He knows exactly what to say and do to make us begin to question God. He has a great influence, but he isn't greater than God. Furthermore, God gives us authority over him. He will not win. The battle has already been won.

While this book is focused on spiritual warfare, it's important to clear up the notion that all suffering and evil is due to warfare. Some suffering is undeserved. However, sometimes what appears as warfare is a consequence for our own sins. In those cases, we must repent and confess. Sometimes God needs to get our attention to draw us closer to him. Sometimes God allows suffering to strengthen, refine, and prepare us for a special assignment He has for us. Don't fall into the trap of self-pity. Like Job in the Bible, you may have been selected for testing. Accept help. Trust God. Sometimes suffering comes from natural consequences from living in a fallen world. This won't last forever. The reason behind the suffering could also be unknown. Wait on God.

But some of the time, it is truly an attack by Satan. We are often left wondering why we had to suffer. You may find yourself asking, "Lord, why am I being hit so intensely and frequently?" Again, as with Job, others may have their theories as to why you are suffering, but only God truly knows. Remember, it is better to know God than to know the why. Trusting God without an explanation from Him might be the most challenging life test. Continue to trust God anyway. Never question his decisions. It is more important to ask God for direction than to ask why something is happening.

This book discusses the tribulations that come because you are a believer, because you have accepted Christ as your savior, and because God has gifted and ordained you as a light in this world. You will be attacked, and there will be an increase in the intensity of these attacks. Any person committed to God should expect Satan's attacks and sneaky moves. Think like a chess player. Be prepared to engage in the game, under God's direction. Be fully armored in God's word, prayer, and praise. This is just the beginning of your countermove.

There is a key point worth emphasizing: There are times you must fight. Ask God to fight the battle with you or for you. I fought various battles and realized nothing was really changing. I had become powerless and things were becoming unmanageable. I needed God to fix things and restore my health, strength, and sanity. He was the power far greater than me. He does eventually fix things. As soon as I surrender and turn it over to him, he fixes things in a way my mind could not comprehend. While our battles are grand and overwhelming to us, they are on a small scale to God. Invite him in. Also, before sin enters our hearts and actions, there is usually a desire, stronghold, or temptation. Don't let these wrongful desires take root.

Prompt 2: Summarize what you just read regarding why warfare takes place. Write about a challenging season in your life that felt like warfare. Did you blame the person or dynamics of the situation and not factor in the unseen realm?

How did God bring you out of that season? In what ways did it work out for your good? Can you see now how that season prepared you for a breakthrough? Are you satisfied with how you responded during that season? Were you properly armored up in prayer, scripture, and praise?

_____

_____

_____

_____

_____

_____

_____

_____

_____

_____

_____

_____

_____

_____

_____

Go back to Day 1 and adjust your battle plan

And pray in the Spirit on all occasions with all kinds of prayers and requests. With this in mind, **be alert and always keep on praying for all the Lord's people**.

- Ephesians 6:18 (NIV)

But when you pray, go into your room, close the door and pray to your Father, who is unseen. Then your Father, who sees **what is done in secret**, will reward you.

- Matthew 6:6 (NIV)

When you fast, do not look somber as the hypocrites do, for they disfigure their faces to show others they are fasting. Truly I tell you, they have received their reward in full. But when you fast, put oil on your head and wash your face, **so that it will not be obvious to others that you are fasting, but only to your Father**, who is unseen; and your Father, who sees what is done in secret, will reward you.

- Matthew 6:16-18 (NIV)

DAY 3

Prayer and Fasting

Prayer and fasting is a weapon for divine intervention. Prayer changes everything. Even when we don't have the strength to pray, God hears our cries and groans as well. Spend time with God. Talk to him regularly. Intercede for other believers. Get on your knees, joined together, and plead out loud. Nothing is impossible with prayer. It is a safeguard. You know the enemy is coming to attack your strength, weakness, or area of greatest influence, so armor up with prayer. Ask God for wisdom and revelation. Rebuke the enemy. Cast him down. Cry out to God. Pray over your loved ones. Say his name with conviction: Jesus!

Warfare Prayer

God, I am asking you to step in
Hear my cry, oh God
Lord please stop my enemies in their steps
I rebuke any demonic influences
Work on my behalf sweet Jesus
Do the impossible
Solicit your angels God
Let me remember my authority through you
Let me remember that I am never alone
You are always with me
Protect me from the enemy's traps God

Show me the warning signs beforehand
Give me strength when they discredit my name
Use me to carry out your glory
Shield me
Envelop me in your arms
Comfort me
Whisper in my ear
What's next God?
Help me to remain obedient
I have nothing to fear
I rebuke every negative spirit Lord
Because you are with me
Every tongue that rises against me
Shall be condemned
Allow me to remain humble
Armor me up Jesus
In prayer, your Holy word, and
By praising and honoring you
Let me remember your promises
Help me to prepare a battle plan
Give me discernment.
Sensitivity to your voice
Let my words be measured
Open my eyes
To the enemy's tactics
Let me turn away from sin
Please God fight my battles for me
Give me the power to defeat the enemy
I need you now
Grant me deliverance from the strongholds in my life
Give me a moment of rest
Let me not succumb to the attacks
In my areas of strength and weakness,
And in my areas of greatest influence
Help me to not give up

Build me up for the battle God
Do what only you can do
As my strength is limited
Let the warfare make me wiser
Not weaker
Nor take me under
Amen

Fasting:

Now let's discuss fasting. Fasting involves voluntarily abstaining from certain pleasures, oftentimes food. It is a submission of our flesh. During this time, increase your prayer and focus on the spirit. Consider praying hourly. It is a time to draw nearer to God and to increase our faith and the power of our prayers.

Fasting is for a purpose. It intensifies prayer and sets you up to receive more from God. We often forget the sacrifice that is involved when asking God for a breakthrough. This demonstrates our yearning for God.

Fasting is an experience that can produce miracles. It humbles us and reminds us of our dependence on God, and prepares us for His response. Expect healing in your area of prayer, a renewed focus on God, and answered prayers. There are certain things that can only come to pass or be revealed through fasting and prayer. Fasting should also extend out to doing good for others.

There are various types of fasts, so do your research and do what works for you. Maybe it's food, maybe it's from various distractions in your life. No matter which fast you adhere to, plan on giving more of your time to God.

Prompt 3: How much time are you authentically spending with God? Is it out of obligation, or are you taking time to pray—and not just to ask for things, but also to express gratitude for all he has done? Take notice of the patterns in your life. What tends to happen when you talk to God consistently? If you can't remember, maybe it's time to refresh your prayer life. What are you willing to commit to? God will bring you back to him in one way or another. You must spend time with him. Are you hindering the effectiveness of your prayers by your behavior? Are you ready to do a fast, whether it is food or a distraction in your life? Are you ready to exercise this discipline, make the sacrifice, and reconnect to God on a deeper level? Are you hungry for Him? What is the connection between spiritual warfare, prayer, and fasting?

_____

_____

_____

_____

_____

_____

_____

_____

_____

_____

_____

_____

Go back to Day 1 and adjust your battle plan

For the word of God is **alive and active**. Sharper than any double-edged sword, it penetrates even to dividing soul and spirit, joints and marrow; it judges the thoughts and attitudes of the heart.

- Hebrews 4:12 (NIV)

DAY 4

Scripture and Biblical Examples

The word of God is a primary weapon of warfare. It provides us with truth to overcome the enemy's lies. It is important to read the Bible consistently, as God tends to reveal things to us through the reading of his word. It is a roadmap. It gives us hope and reminds us of God's love. It allows us to align our thoughts with God's word.

Being in the presence of God and studying and meditating on his word is a priority. It is truly nourishment for our soul. It gives us strength. It keeps us on track and attuned to good versus evil. Make some time to be alone with the word of God daily. Through the reading, we learn more about who God is. Don't just read arbitrarily. Meditate on his word. Ask God to lead you to the areas of the Bible he wants you to focus on, and to help you to extract personal meaning from what you read.

The following are three important scriptures as you face warfare:

Warfare Scripture 1: Psalm 91 (NIV)

Whoever dwells in the shelter of the Most High
    will rest in the shadow of the Almighty.
    I will say of the Lord, "He is my refuge and my fortress,
    my God, in whom I trust."
Surely he will save you
    from the fowler's snare
    and from the deadly pestilence.

He will cover you with his feathers,
>   and under his wings you will find refuge;
>   his faithfulness will be your shield and rampart.
You will not fear the terror of night,
>   nor the arrow that flies by day,
nor the pestilence that stalks in the darkness,
>   nor the plague that destroys at midday.
A thousand may fall at your side,
>   ten thousand at your right hand,
>   but it will not come near you.
You will only observe with your eyes
>   and see the punishment of the wicked.
If you say, "The Lord is my refuge,"
>   and you make the Most High your dwelling,
no harm will overtake you,
>   no disaster will come near your tent.
For he will command his angels concerning you
>   to guard you in all your ways;
they will lift you up in their hands,
>   so that you will not strike your foot against a stone.
You will tread on the lion and the cobra;
>   you will trample the great lion and the serpent.
"Because he loves me," says the Lord, "I will rescue him;
>   I will protect him, for he acknowledges my name.
He will call on me, and I will answer him;
>   I will be with him in trouble,
>   I will deliver him and honor him.
With long life I will satisfy him
>   and show him my salvation."

Warfare Scripture 2: Psalm 23 (NIV)

The Lord is my shepherd, I lack nothing.
He makes me lie down in green pastures,

he leads me beside quiet waters,
he refreshes my soul.
He guides me along the right paths
for his name's sake.
Even though I walk
through the darkest valley,
I will fear no evil,
for you are with me;
your rod and your staff,
they comfort me.
You prepare a table before me
in the presence of my enemies.
You anoint my head with oil;
my cup overflows.
Surely your goodness and love will follow me
all the days of my life,
and I will dwell in the house of the Lord
forever.

Warfare Scripture 3: Psalm 121 (NIV)

I lift up my eyes to the mountains—
where does my help come from?
My help comes from the Lord,
the Maker of heaven and earth.
He will not let your foot slip—
he who watches over you will not slumber;
indeed, he who watches over Israel
will neither slumber nor sleep.
The Lord watches over you—
the Lord is your shade at your right hand;
the sun will not harm you by day,
nor the moon by night.
The Lord will keep you from all harm—

he will watch over your life;
the Lord will watch over your coming and going
both now and forevermore.

Additionally, it is wise to study examples of those that faced warfare in the Bible. For the Biblical figure Samson, warfare showed up by attacking his greatest strength, and the temptations that come as a result of power and being isolated.

Samson had supernatural strength that no one could defeat. His ability to keep his strength was connected to him never cutting his hair. One night he was seduced by a woman named Delilah. With his defenses down, he revealed this information regarding his hair. He fell into lust. Delilah cut his hair and his strength vanished. The Lord was no longer with Samson. Others were able to defeat Samson and put him in jail. Over time, his hair grew back, as did his strength. Despite what appeared to be a mistake, God still used these circumstances to fulfill his purpose.

Prompt 4: How often are you opening up your Bible? We have to be armored up with scripture. What do you notice when you consistently read the word of God? What happens when you don't consistently read His word? Name a specific time God has spoken to you in the past through the reading of His word? Remember, God will bring you back to him in one way or another. You must spend time with him. You must allow him to reveal certain things to you through the reading of the Bible.

Reflect on the three scriptures above. How are these scriptures resonating with you? How does the reading of the Bible connect to spiritual warfare? What can we glean from the story of Samson? What are some other biblical examples of warfare?

_____

_____

_____

_____

_____

_____

_____

_____

_____

_____

_____

_____

_____

Go back to Day 1 and adjust your battle plan

Submit yourselves, then, to God. **Resist the devil**, and he will flee from you.

- James 4:7 (NIV)

DAY 5

Praise and Worship

Worship is an expression of God's love. When we sing, we tend to focus only on the song, amplifying God's greatness, momentarily forgetting our sorrows. Every time you praise God, there is a change within you or your circumstances. Things begin to happen in the unseen realm. Praise opens up miracles.

Praise and worship draw us nearer to God. Praise is the conduit for God to put something new in us. Praise God in the midst of the storm. Worship your way through. Praise God in advance for answering your prayers. Praise him at all times. In the Bible, as David was running away from Saul, he was still praising God.

Praise him in worship and song, with joy and thanksgiving, deep in your heart. In everything, give thanks. God is good! Our problems will not last forever! Worship God boldly and exuberantly.

In the midst of your tribulation, continue to praise God, even when tempted to complain. I recall a time when I was extremely sick. I still don't know what was wrong. I was so defeated. I had been sick on and off for two years. I began wondering, *Why am I here? I just keep getting sick.* I was beginning to believe there was a problem with me. Negativity took over me as I shivered in bed, sweating, shaking, feeling weak, and unable to eat. The Holy Spirit spoke to me and I kept repeating, "Courage, faith, surrender," but with positive expectancy and hope. That was ALL I had in that moment. My faith and the quiet rejoicing released a great amount of power. That night my husband went back out in the snow for the third time to get me more medicine. When I eventually went to the hospital, my brother and friend showed up to provide support. The next day my mom brought me a special soup, and I was healed. In the next month I was overflowing with blessings. Despite this health-related tribulation, I kept the faith, and God had angels show up in various forms, just when I needed them. Praise and worship got me through that ordeal.

In retrospect, I believe that particular tribulation was a wake-up call for me to control some of the judgments of others that I had allowed in my mind. It drew me back to my knowing that judgment was wrong and that I was dependent on God. Praising God despite my circumstances seemed to trigger a supernatural healing.

You must exalt God. He is great! He is worthy to be praised. Begin your day with solid praise and worship and your day will never be the same. Exalt God consistently and see what happens.

Praise Poem

Lord,
Seldom words describe
Your love
Miraculous intentional
Savior
Detailed
Master creator
The prescribed purpose you have set out for our lives
Healer
Comforter
Protector
Burden bearer
Energizer
Hope giver
Vindicator
Battle fighter
Meeter of all needs

Source of strength in times of weariness
The everything, the everywhere
The help in times of trouble
Prince of peace, Lord of Lords
The forgiver of sins
The orchestrator of all good things
God there is no description to adequately capture your magnitude
Your commitment to your promises
The love you have for us
Grace and mercy giver
Blessings supplier
The joy
The gratitude
Moments of splendor
The gifts
The anointing
The peace
The trust
God, why?
Why do you love us so deeply? And so intensely? We are so undeserving
Unconditional
L-O-V-E
Steady, firm, and rooted
Thank you, God,
We praise your name
Thank you, God
We glorify you. We honor you. Thank you, God,
You alone are worthy to be praised

Prompt 5: How has your praise life been lately? Reflect on this notion of carving out time on a daily basis to praise God for who he is, not for a want or desire, just for being the amazing God that he is. Reflect on a time you praised your way through a storm. How does praise and worship connect to warfare?

_____

_____

_____

_____

_____

_____

_____

_____

_____

_____

_____

_____

_____

_____

_____

_____

Go back to Day 1 and adjust your battle plan

The one who does what is sinful is of the devil, because the devil has been sinning from the beginning. The reason the Son of God appeared was to **destroy the devil's work**.

- 1 John 3:8 (NIV)

DAY 6

Follow the Prompting of the Holy Spirit and Obey

Call on God for guidance and he will lead us through the prompting of the Holy Spirit. He will provide step by step guidance. Ask, "How do I handle this Lord? What have I not said or done? Do I step back? Do I step up? What should I do? Lead me God. Should I make the phone call? Apply to the job?" He will meet you at your point of need and steer you in the right direction. God is always near even if he seems silent.

One of the most powerful moments is when you begin to know and recognize God's voice in situations. When I am not at peace with something, that can't be God, so I wait until I get a clear message.

The Holy Spirit is that still small voice that will remind you of scripture, a memory of the past, etc. Anything to recall what is right for you in that moment. For me, it's my inner compass that tells me, "Yes, my child, do that. Say that"; "My child, not right now. I will tell you when"; "My child, now is a good time to apologize"; "My child, this is the sacrifice I need from you right now"; or "My child, do not be hurt. Do not be offended. I'm with you. This feeling is temporary. It will pass."

I remember God distinctly telling me who my spouse was, to continue pursuing certain job opportunities, where to move, when to try for a baby, etc. He is our GPS, our true compass. Obey God and prosper. Learn to recognize his voice by spending time with him.

Prompt 6: Reflect on your sensitivity to the Holy Spirit. Are you aware of when God is speaking to you and guiding you? Have you been obedient? Recall a distinct moment you went against the prompting. How did that work out? Recall a time you followed the Holy Spirit. How did that work out? What is the connection between following the prompting of the Holy Spirit and warfare?

_____

_____

_____

_____

_____

_____

_____

_____

_____

_____

_____

_____

_____

_____

_____

_____

Go back to Day 1 and adjust your battle plan

And when you stand praying, **if you hold anything against anyone, forgive them**, so that your Father in heaven may forgive you your sins.

- Mark 11:25 (NIV)

DAY 7

Forgiveness

Forgiveness is a weapon against spiritual warfare. In the human experience people say and do things that are hurtful and offensive. But why hold on to anger against that person when it isn't about that person? Some people don't even realize they are being used to betray you. We take our unfavorable experiences and our minds become filled with various thoughts and emotions toward a person, group of people, or institution. Meanwhile, none of their actions are personal. There is a battle going on, and Satan will use these offenses to cause division among us. There are principalities in action causing hurt, conflict, and disruption.

Furthermore, the enemy accesses certain people more than others. He often accesses people through their traumas, wounds, and insecurities. It's better to whisper a prayer for that person and move forward in forgiveness, than to stay in the swirl of negative emotions. Once we realize we are not fighting a person, we can more easily extend grace, mercy, and forgiveness. Refuse to assist the devil by harboring unforgiveness. Forgive immediately.

Prompt 7: Have you been harboring unforgiveness? You cannot expect God to forgive you if you have not forgiven others. What steps can you take to move in the direction of forgiveness? How is unforgiveness connected to warfare?

_____

_____

_____

_____

_____

_____

_____

_____

_____

_____

_____

_____

_____

_____

_____

_____

Go back to Day 1 and adjust your battle plan

Bring the whole tithe into the storehouse, that there may be food in my house. Test me in this," says the LORD Almighty, "and see if I will not **throw open the floodgates of heaven and pour out so much blessing that there will not be room enough to store it**.

- Malachi 3:10 (NIV)

DAY 8

Tithes and Offering

We can't place anything above God, including money. We must worship God with our giving. Tithing is a demonstration that God has our heart, so give cheerfully! Tithing also extends the work of the kingdom. Everything belongs to Him. He is asking for our disciplined demonstration of our commitment to him. He is asking for 10% of our earnings to the body of believers that are feeding us spiritually.

When we tithe, our finances are blessed. This is an area of our spiritual life that can be put to the test. In my personal experience, tithing has been a consistent safeguard. When I tithe, I'm alright. When I don't tithe, I am not alright. We can block certain blessings from coming into our life because of our inability to give. The scripture says "and prove me now..." God will show you. Talk to God, and see what happens in your life. God may impress upon your heart to give more.

Yes, you do have enough money to give a tithe and offering. This is not a suggestion to give your entire paycheck away. This is a suggestion to give 10% in tithes and some extra for offering. Offering is an additional giving on top of tithe.

Prompt 8: Reflect on your giving. Have you sacrificed your time and money as a demonstration that God has your heart? Have you been tithing? If you have tithed in the past, what happens when you tithe? What happens when you do not tithe? How is the giving of tithes and offering connected to warfare? How does this habit serve as a layer of protection?

_____

_____

_____

_____

_____

_____

_____

_____

_____

_____

_____

_____

_____

_____

_____

_____

_____

_____

Go back to Day 1 and adjust your battle plan

I have given you authority to trample on snakes and scorpions and to overcome all the power of the enemy; **nothing will harm you**.

- Luke 10:19 (NIV)

DAY 9

Remember God's Promises and Your Authority

In the midst of our battle, we must remember who we are and who we belong to. God has promised us many things. When you reflect on God's promises, one thing that is clear is that we are not alone. He is fighting our battles right alongside us. He is the source of the supernatural strength that helps us to endure. When you are weary, declare the blood of Jesus. Shout out his name.

He is there with us in the storm. He will eventually stop the storm. He sent us to the place and space knowing the storm was coming. But we are his warriors. We are there for his glory and to do his good work. We must always lean on this knowing.

Additionally, God wants us to be confident in the authority he has given us. We don't need to cower in fear when the attacks are plentiful. Tell Satan to flee. Draw on the endless reservoir of strength God makes available to us through Him.

A few of God's promises:

1. BATTLE FIGHTER: God will fight your battles. Just be still. Cry out to him. He will help you when you are in trouble. He will strike down evil people (Deuteronomy 28:7, Exodus 14:14).
2. BLESSINGS: Put God first and things will open up for you (Mathew 6:33). Keep God's commandments and walk in

obedience and he will bless you (Deuteronomy 28:9). Pay your tithe and God will pour out a blessing onto you (Malachi 3:10). When you pray and ask God for something, believe, and you shall receive (Mark 11:24, Psalm 37:4).

3. COMPANIONSHIP: Even in the darkest valley, God never leaves us (Psalm 23:4).

4. COURAGE: Never fear anything. Don't be afraid or discouraged. God is with us. No matter the size of the battle, he will help us when it feels like there is no hope. When afraid, put all your trust in Him (Isaiah 41:10, Isaiah 41:13, Deuteronomy 31:8, Joshua 1:9, Psalm 27:1, 2 Chronicles 20:15).

5. A PLACE IN ETERNITY: Eternity awaits us (2 Peter 3:13).

6. FAITHFULNESS: Prove yourself faithful to God, and he is faithful to you (Psalm 18:25).

7. FORGIVENESS: Confess your sins and God will forgive you (1 John 1:9).

8. HELP: When you pray, God hears you and will help you. (2 Chronicles 7:14).

9. LONG LIFE: Despite their weaknesses, honor your parents and your days will be long (Exodus 20:12).

10. LOVE: God's love is unwavering (Isaiah 54:10).

11. MEETER OF ALL NEEDS: All your needs will be met (Philippians 4:19).

12. PEACE: When chaos abounds, he will give you peace (Isaiah 26:3).

13. PROSPERITY: He has plans for you to prosper and be blessed (Jeremiah 29:11, Psalm 1:1-3).

14. PROTECTION: God is our refuge. No weapon, no evil formed against you shall prosper. Even the "bad" will work for your good. He will make sure you go unharmed no matter how things appear. We can hide in his arms, until trouble has passed (Isaiah 54:17).

15. WISDOM: God will give you wisdom (James 1:5).

16. STRENGTH: He will give you strength when you are weary. Wait on God (Isaiah 40:29, Isaiah 40:31).

17. VICTORY: No matter the difficulty, press on. We will be able to claim victory over our enemies. He fights with us and for us (Isaiah 43:2, Psalm 44:5-7, Joshua 23:10, Psalm 18:3).

And the list goes on and on. When we go against some of the conditional statements like "Honor your parents, and your days will be long," we bring additional tribulations onto ourselves. The warfare is challenging enough, we don't need to add to that in any way by our own misguided actions.

Prompt 9: What is the connection between warfare and God's promises? How does knowing his promises serve as an armor? Which of the above promises resonates with you the most? In what way? What else does God promise us?

_____

_____

_____

_____

_____

_____

_____

_____

_____

_____

_____

_____

_____

_____

_____

Go back to Day 1 and adjust your battle plan

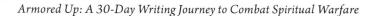

Blessed are the meek, for they will inherit the earth.

- Matthew 5:5 (NIV)

Pride goes before destruction, a haughty spirit before a fall.

- Proverbs 16:18 (NIV)

DAY 10

Monitor Pride

The Enemy

Naive and needy
Never giving God
The credit He deserves
I cleave to the noise
And distraction of man
Obedient to the outrageous
Enemy
Liar
Thief
The offended
The abused
Anxious
Supporter of sin
Promoter of division
Frozen in pain
The victim
The flesh
Lingering distress
The residue of the offense
Doubt
I rebuke thee

Ego
Selfish ego
Make me big
Make them love me
I am in control
It was me
The talents
The gifts
The strength
It was me
Me, me, me
It was all me
Untouchable
Overlooked
Overdue

Any and all success in our life comes from God. We have to be careful of developing a pompous haughty attitude, attributing the goodness in our life to ourselves. Pride is deceptive, especially when things are going right in our lives. It inflates our perception of ourselves. We must give all the honor and glory to God. When we begin to congratulate ourselves for things, we have to be careful pride, self-righteousness, or arrogance is not setting in. Pride can show up as looking at others and wondering how they are so blessed: "Why am I not getting those accolades and the promotion?" Believe that God will exalt you if he wants you in a certain position. Pride may show up as looking at others in judgment and condemnation: "Why isn't someone a particular way?" Pride may also show up when we do things for show or praise from others.

Sometimes tribulation comes because of our own pride. In the Bible, the Pharisees were also considered people who were filled with pride. Satan became corrupt through his own pride, so imagine what pride does to us. Pride is major.

When I am prideful and my ego and flesh are involved, I am usually angry or boastful in an unhealthy way. I might be giving advice that I am not even following myself. I might hold onto anger and not forgive. I might come across as an arrogant know-it-all, losing patience too easily for those who don't meet a set criterion. When prideful, the focus is only on self. We have to constantly self-assess. Pride is present somewhere if I am complaining, blaming, trying to gain something over others, envious, bitter, easily offended, not trusting God and believing he is the source of good, seeking revenge, or focusing on the faults or deficiencies in others.

There is a saying, "There is always pride before the fall," or "Haughtiness leads to destruction," meaning that before we are humbled by God, we are usually in a state of being puffed up and filled with ego. We may feel we are invincible or untouchable.

Humility means proper respect for God for all he has done. Remain mellow, in a state of gratitude, and God-focused, not self-focused. Focus on God's blessings and not what we perceive to be our own doing. Be humble, meek, and submissive when God tells you to be.

Remain in a holy state, without the dominance of the flesh. Learn to play second fiddle and focus on others. Live a life of servanthood. When we focus our attention not on ourselves, but on helping and affirming others, we are more aligned with humility.

Prompt 10: Reflect on the notion of humility and meekness. In what ways have you demonstrated humility lately? How about pride, self-righteousness, or arrogance? How can you bring yourself to focus on God and all He has done? Can we shift from self-praise and inflation to a place of gratitude to God?

_____

_____

_____

_____

_____

_____

_____

_____

_____

_____

_____

_____

_____

_____

_____

_____

_____

_____

Go back to Day 1 and adjust your battle plan

Therefore, **confess your sins to each other and pray for each other so that you may be healed**. The prayer of a righteous person is powerful and effective.

- James 5:16. (NIV)

As **iron sharpens iron**, so one person sharpens another.

- Proverbs 27:17 (NIV)

For where two or three gather in my name, **there am I with them**.

- Matthew 18:20 (NIV)

Though one may be overpowered, two can defend themselves. **A cord of three strands is not quickly broken.**

- Ecclesiastes 4:12 (NIV)

Walk with the wise and become wise, for a companion of fools suffers harm.

- Proverbs 13:20 (NIV)

The righteous choose their friends carefully, but the way of the wicked leads them astray.

--Proverbs 12:26 (NIV)

DAY 11

Connect with Other Believers

Join forces with the People of God—Enlist the prayer and encouragement of other believers when under attack. The people in your ear and advising you should always be the right people, as they can stray you toward God or toward the enemy. Always remember, this is kingdom work.

There are certain blessings and insights that can only come from a body of believers. Don't underestimate this power. The battle is challenging, and even more challenging when fought alone. If you are attuned to the Holy Spirit, he will guide you as to who is a spiritual ally and times you should walk the journey alone.

Oftentimes it takes one or two believers to lead the fight, and to demonstrate enough courage to wage the war against the enemy. Some believers know there is wrong or injustice but lack the courage to fight. Try not to be disappointed in them. Not everyone is there yet on their journey. Give them that allowance. Their prayers might be what they have to give at this moment.

Prompt 11: Who are your advisors? Who are you following? Do you have a body of believers that can stand in the gap? When you are worn down and weary, who can intercede and pray for you? Reflect on a time you combined with other believers to fight for the glory of God. If you are not there yet to lead the charge for justice, can you follow other leaders who are doing what is right?

_____

_____

_____

_____

_____

_____

_____

_____

_____

_____

_____

_____

_____

_____

_____

_____

_____

Go back to Day 1 and adjust your battle plan

Finally, brothers and sisters, whatever is true, whatever is noble, whatever is right, whatever is pure, whatever is lovely, whatever is admirable—**if anything is excellent or praiseworthy—think about such things**.

- Philippians 4:8 (NIV)

DAY 12

Monitor What Is Feeding Your Spirit

Feed your spirit with Godly things. What do you watch? Who or what do you listen to? What is taking up your time? It is best that it is aligned to Godly principles, because it will influence your thoughts and actions. That doesn't mean you should only listen to or watch particular programs if you have interest elsewhere, but be aware of the distribution of your time. Time is our most precious commodity. If the majority of your time is being spent with ungodly things and other distractions, how much time is being allocated to God? How much time is being allocated to your purpose?

Prompt 12: What have you been allowing in, through the things you are watching in your spare time or through various media outlets? Remove the distractions. What are you listening to? What is feeding your spirit? Who is feeding your spirit? Is it purposeful or purposeless?

_____

_____

_____

_____

_____

_____

_____

_____

_____

_____

_____

_____

_____

_____

_____

_____

_____

_____

Go back to Day 1 and adjust your battle plan

Love is patient, love is kind. It does not envy, it does not boast, it is not proud. It does not dishonor others, it is not self-seeking, it is not easily angered, **it keeps no record of wrongs**.

- 1 Corinthians 13:4-5 (NIV)

DAY 13

Love the People in Front of You

The people who arrive in our lives have been sent by God for a reason. We are to pay attention and love the people in front of us on a daily basis, including our family. This is our greatest life mission.

What does love look like? Love is a verb. It is about doing. Sacrifice. Support. Being a source of happiness. Giving your attention, time, and money to help, encourage, be affectionate toward others, offer a smile or other gesture of happiness and care toward our fellow man. Be happy when they are happy and compassionate when they are sad. Offer gifts and tokens of love towards them during celebratory moments in their lives. Be a resource, especially when you have a gift that they lack. Love is also seeing their pain even in the midst of your own pain. It's loving even when the other person is unlovable, which is an exercise in patience.

Often, we don't feel like loving certain people, especially when they behave badly. This is often the time they need to be loved the most. Don't mistreat people, even if they mistreat you. The Bible says, "Love endureth all things."

There are five love languages, and loving people means sprinkling a bit of all the love languages toward them and eventually identifying what is their particular love language(s) and applying it. What does the person need from me to feel loved? Let me pay attention to that person and do the things that make the person feel validated and filled up. The five love languages include: Words of Affirmation, Acts of Service, Receiving Gifts, Quality Time, and Physical Touch.

Love can be as simple as showing up, sending a text or a card, or greeting someone by name with a smile. It's the small daily caring touch points. It is not self-serving. It is the act of giving and sacrifice. That is love. God is love. Seek out people who are presently in need of love and love them. Appreciate those who have shown love toward you.

It is important to note, at this point, the importance of boundaries. We can love and have self-respect simultaneously. Some may try to take advantage of our kindness. It's more challenging to battle the storms of life when people set out to use and abuse us. Love also knows when to step back because entangling with you and your unresolved pain could be a detriment to both of us. Lack of proper boundaries is its own warfare.

Prompt 13: What are ways that you have demonstrated love lately? What was the last loving thing someone did for you? How did it make you feel? What sacrifices have you made lately for others? What loving boundaries need to be put in place?

_____

_____

_____

_____

_____

_____

_____

_____

_____

_____

_____

_____

_____

_____

_____

_____

_____

_____

Go back to Day 1 and adjust your battle plan

Now to him who is able **to do immeasurably more than all we ask or imagine,** according to his power that is at work within us.

- Ephesians 3:20 (NIV)

DAY 14

Gratitude

Gratitude means really reflecting on all the blessings in your life and thanking God for them. It's also paying attention to the small things, like seeing the sunrise, finding a parking spot, enjoying a warm cup of tea. Gratitude can show up as being satisfied with your blessings, your lot. No comparisons.

There seems to be a connection between the qualities of gratitude, forgiveness and humility. When I am upset with a person, if I shift to focus on their admirable qualities, how they have been a blessing in the past, and what I appreciate and why I am grateful for that person, I can suppress my pride and forgive them. I can take the first step to reach out and reconcile. Gratitude redirects you to what matters.

Be grateful for everything. EVERYTHING. Try even to be grateful for pain, because it serves a purpose. We can learn to live and love differently based on the unfavorable situations we overcome.

Prompt 14: List two things you are grateful for, and give three details for each item you list. Explain in those three details why you are grateful. Be specific. What is working in your life right now? How is the universe conspiring on your behalf? Reflect on a recent miracle or full circle moment you experienced. Reflect on a recent loving moment. Consider how a painful experience from the past also resulted in blessings. Thank God for it all. How can gratitude act as a weapon against warfare?

_____

_____

_____

_____

_____

_____

_____

_____

_____

_____

_____

_____

_____

_____

_____

Go back to Day 1 and adjust your battle plan

Do not be anxious about anything, but in every situation, by prayer and petition, with thanksgiving, **present your requests to God**.

- Philippians 4:6 (NIV)

DAY 15

Be Patient and Wait Well

Waiting well is one of the most challenging things in life. We feel stuck and at a standstill. It feels as though God is not hearing our pleas. He's giving us no signs of what is next; however, during this time, he is building our faith.

Even Jesus had to wait on God, so don't expect God to move in our own timing. Remain at peace. Be patient. Be your best in your current place and space. Minimize complaining. Wait and see what God has in store. Ask God to comfort you in his arms as you wait on an answer from him.

The warfare can feel like it is designed to take you under in despair. When he does respond, it can feel like we are going backwards. We become devastated. We have to wait once again for any progress forward. Little do we know that what appears to be a step backwards is a set up to propel us forward in his due time. You will never be able to see that in the place that you are currently in. Stand firm.

What many of us have learned in life is that His timing really and truly is the best timing. Any blessing that comes too soon, is not a blessing. I don't know about you, but I would rather be in the right God-ordained conditions for my blessing. What has your name on it, is coming to you. Wait on God.

Prompt 15: Has God made you wait before? Recall how agonizing that was. What did you learn during that time? What were the lessons during the waiting season? Did you use the waiting season to heal and transform, or to complain? What is the connection between patience and warfare?

_____

_____

_____

_____

_____

_____

_____

_____

_____

_____

_____

_____

_____

_____

_____

_____

_____

_____

Go back to Day 1 and adjust your battle plan

All of us also lived among them at one time, gratifying the cravings of our flesh and following its desires and thoughts. Like the rest, we were by nature deserving of wrath.

-Ephesians 2:3 (NIV)

The acts of the sinful nature are obvious: sexual immorality, impurity and debauchery; idolatry and witchcraft; hatred, discord, jealousy, fits of rage, selfish ambition, dissensions, factions and envy; drunkenness, orgies, and the like. I warn you, as I did before, that those who live like this will not inherit the kingdom of God.

- Galatians 5:19-21 (NIV)

The prudent see danger and take refuge, but the simple keep going and pay the penalty.

- Proverbs 22:3 (NIV)

DAY 16

Be Mindful of the Flesh

We all battle with the flesh and our selfish desires for instant gratification. It's an everyday battle. It comes with being human. If you live according to your desires and impulses without factoring in the morality of the situation, you are living out of the flesh. We all have fleshly desires, and the enemy sets traps to attack this area of weakness. Wanting something we don't need or which will get us in trouble, is the flesh. Wanting the accolades and for people to affirm us or to feel we are in power, is the flesh. Anger and deep agitation is the flesh. Fussing, fighting, jealousy, envy, the pull of addiction, and other strongholds is all the flesh.

It's like a tug of war with the spirit and the flesh. The enemy seeks out ways to tempt us, while the spirit wants us to focus on Christ and doing what is morally right. Things of the flesh are a distraction to shift our focus from God and onto our wants. If you are feeling of the flesh, you must take a step back and reflect. Is this my flesh? Is this my ego? God, what do you want me to do in this situation that is pleasing to you?

Prompt 16: Who is winning the tug of war in your life right now, the spirit or the flesh? The battle only intensifies when we are living in the flesh. What is the connection between warfare and the flesh?

_____

_____

_____

_____

_____

_____

_____

_____

_____

_____

_____

_____

_____

_____

_____

_____

_____

Go back to Day 1 and adjust your battle plan

You, dear children, are from God and have overcome them, because the one who is in you is greater than the one who is in the world.

- 1 John 4:4 (NIV)

Do not love the world or anything in the world. If anyone loves the world, love for the Father is not in them. For everything in the world—the lust of the flesh, the lust of the eyes, and the pride of life—comes not from the Father but from the world. The world and its desires pass away, but **whoever does the will of God lives forever**.

-1 John 2:15-17 (NIV)

Do not conform to the pattern of this world, but **be transformed by the renewing of your mind.** Then you will be able to test and approve what God's will is-his good, pleasing and perfect will.

- Romans 12:2 (NIV)

No temptation has overtaken you except what is common to mankind. And **God is faithful**; he will not let you be tempted beyond what you can bear. **But when you are tempted, he will also provide a way out so that you can endure it.**

- 1 Corinthians 10:13 (NIV)

DAY 17

Be Mindful of the World

Similar to the flesh, being of the world is also an everyday battle. It is valuing the "things" of this world. This includes living for money, fame, power, degrees, titles—in other words, anything other than Christ. There is nothing wrong with wanting achievement, but what is the driving force behind your pursuit of these things? Is it for God's glory?

Although we are living in the world, we should aim not to be in it, valuing the pursuit of things over the pursuit of God. Don't boast about worldly accomplishments. They come and they go. Be a humble servant. Do everything to the glory of God. Make sure you prioritize getting to know God and remaining close to him so the pressures of keeping up in the world don't overtake you.

To not be of this world means to fight for God's glory. I must intentionally choose Christ's way daily, moving by God's leadership and relying on God to be my compass. We are the walking, talking representations of Jesus in this fallen world. Are we living up to that responsibility?

Prompt 17: What is the connection between being of the world and warfare? In what ways are you living of this world? Are you fixated on "things"? How can we live in this world but not be of this world?

Go back to Day 1 and adjust your battle plan

We demolish arguments and every pretension that sets itself up against the knowledge of God, and we take captive every thought to **make it obedient to Christ**.

-2 Corinthians 10:5 (NIV)

DAY 18

Be Attuned to the Common Attacks

Each attack is an opportunity to pivot your attention to something that matters, is meaningful, and needs your attention.

Pass the test. Beat the devil at his own game. Bypass this current distraction. You have important work to do.

The enemy recognizes when you walk in your purpose, and that is perceived as a threat. He will therefore launch attacks in one or more areas of your life. Don't allow the enemy to allow you to waste your life with these unproductive things.

Remember, the enemy only attacks what's valuable.

Here are some common tactics adopted by the enemy:

1. ABANDONMENT/ISOLATION
2. ABUSE
3. ABUSE OF POWER
4. ACCUSATIONS OF INADEQUACY
5. ADDICTIONS
6. ALTERATION OF OUTCOMES
7. ANXIETY
8. APATHY
9. ATTACK ON RELATIONSHIPS
10. BAD LUCK
11. BAD NEWS

12. BEING OF THE WORLD
13. BETRAYAL
14. BLAME/GUILT
15. BOMBARD WITH ATTACKS
16. BULLIES
17. CHAOS
18. COMMUNICATION STRUGGLES
19. COMPARISON
20. CONFUSION
21. CRITICISM
22. DEATH (spiritual)
23. DECEPTION
24. DEFAMATION
25. DEFICIENCIES
26. DELAY/FRUSTRATE
27. DEPRESSION
28. DESTRUCTION
29. DIMINISH YOUR EXISTENCE
30. DISAPPOINTMENT/DISSATISFACTION
31. DISCORD
32. DISCOURAGEMENT
33. DISHARMONY/UNREST
34. DISRUPTIONS
35. DISTRACTIONS
36. DISTURBANCES
37. DIVISION
38. DOUBT
39. EMBARRASSMENT
40. EVERYTHING HAPPENING AT ONCE
41. EVIL DEMONIC SPIRITS
42. FALSE ACCUSATIONS
43. FALSE ALLIANCES
44. FALSE FLATTERY
45. FEAR
46. FINANCIAL ISSUES

47. FOCUS ON YOUR INSECURITIES
48. GAMES
49. GENERATIONAL CURSES
50. HARSH WORDS
51. HURT FEELINGS
52. IGNORED/NEGLECTED
53. IMPRISONMENT
54. INFESTATION
55. INFIDELITY
56. INJURY
57. INSULTS
58. INTIMIDATION
59. ISOLATION
60. JEALOUSY
61. LACK OF APOLOGY OR REMORSE
62. LACK OF PROTECTION OR SUPPORT
63. LACK OF THINGS YOU NEED
64. LIES
65. LUST
66. MEAN WORDS/ ACTIONS
67. MISINFORMATION
68. NEGATIVE THINKING
69. NIGHTMARES (Of your worst fears)
70. OVERLY SENSITIVE
71. OVERWORKED
72. POWER STRUGGLES
73. PRE-BLESSING WARFARE
74. PROMISCUITY
75. PULLED INTO SIN BY PEERS
76. QUESTION GOD
77. REJECTION
78. SABOTAGE
79. SCARCITY
80. SEASON OF LOSS
81. SEDUCTION

82. SICKNESS
83. STIR UP EMOTIONS
84. STRENGTH, WEAKNESS, INFLUENCE, and BROKENNESS (attacks)
85. STRESS
86. STRIFE
87. STRONGHOLDS
88. STUBBORNESS
89. TAKE ADVANTAGE OF YOUR NAIVETY
90. TAUNT/MAKE FUN OF
91. TEMPTATION
92. TRAPS
93. TURMOIL
94. UNEASY/UNBALANCED
95. UNFAIR TREATMENT
96. UNFOCUSED
97. USERS
98. WASTED TIME
99. WORRY
100. WRATH

Prompt 18: Which of these tactics by the enemy resonates with you? Knowing is half the battle. How is the enemy currently testing you? Are you armored up for this battle?

_____

_____

_____

_____

_____

_____

_____

_____

_____

_____

_____

_____

_____

_____

_____

_____

_____

Go back to Day 1 and adjust your battle plan

My enemies turn back; they stumble and perish before you.

- Psalm 9:3 (NIV)

Then my enemies will turn back when I call for help. By this I will know that **God is for me.**

- Psalm 56:9 (NIV)

My God on whom I can rely. God will go before me and will let me gloat over those who slander me.

- Psalm 59:10 (NIV)

All my enemies will be overwhelmed with shame and anguish; they will turn back and suddenly be put to shame.

- Psalm 6:10 (NIV)

DAY 19

Overcome Betrayal

There is one satanic attack that we are going to circle back to that impacts our relationships, and that is betrayal. Betrayal hurts. It's hard for someone to hurt you unless you love or care about them or have established trust in some way. This is why betrayal is a tough one. Betrayal means breaking an unspoken bond between individuals.

You have poured your heart into a person or a group of people, and then not only do they not show up for you, but the even appear to be spearheading the fight against you. It stings. It is sometimes from those who you would least expect this behavior. It seems as though the enemy has taken root in them. It can be quite shocking and devastating.

Betrayal could be in the form of jealousy and pretending to be for you. Betrayal can show up as mistreatment or taking the opposing side of a situation. Betrayal has an interesting way of backfiring. I've never seen someone deliberately try to do harm or go against the good and then thrive afterward.

Judas and others betrayed Jesus. We should expect betrayal in this life; however, know that there is redemption after betrayal! We are human and make mistakes. Additionally, human relationships are complicated, and what can be perceived as betrayal by one can be perceived differently by the other person.

Rest assured, some of the key people that betrayed you will seek to redeem themselves from the offense in the future. They might make attempts to prove that they are sorry. Forgive them. That is what grace is all about. Refer back to forgiveness. Erect boundaries if you need to. Remember, the battle is not with man. Don't waste time on low-level demons and offenses. Wait for the big demons. Just step back and watch. Make forgiveness automatic after you have been betrayed. It was the principality working within that person, not that person themself. Remember that it is all a blessing—the good, the bad, and the betrayal. This person may not be intended to go with you into your next season of life. Let go and let God lead.

Prompt 19: Do you need to forgive someone that betrayed you? How is betrayal by loved ones connected to warfare? The armor of grace and forgiveness is key when overcoming betrayal.

_____

_____

_____

_____

_____

_____

_____

_____

_____

_____

_____

_____

_____

_____

_____

_____

_____

Go back to Day 1 and adjust your battle plan

Wait for the LORD; be strong and take heart and wait for the LORD.
-Psalm 27:14 (NIV)

DAY 20

Remain Steadfast with Faith

Faith is believing what we don't see. Often times it is difficult to see ourselves out of our current circumstances. Despite what external circumstances tell us, we have to believe God can do what he says he will do. We don't know how God will get us out. That is where faith steps in. If there is anything in this battle plan you must do immediately, that is to enlarge your faith. We have to be still and remember who God is. He is still on the throne. He will work all things out for our good. TRUST that he will get you through it. TRUST that he will use whatever we endure to glorify his name. All things work together for good. ALL THINGS. There is opportunity wrapped in every storm. There is purpose for our pain. God can turn our persecution into a victory.

We are often toggling between fear/stress and faith at any given time, but there is no need to fear. When God moves, we will know it was God. Pray. Trust God. Act as if it is so. Have aggressive expectations. Have faith he will see you through. Has he ever abandoned you before? God will protect you. There is no need to retaliate. He is an on-time God. Rejoice even in the midst of adversities. Keep your eyes focused on Him at all times. Take things one step at a time, one whisper from God at a time.

When family members are sick, we have to have faith they will get better. When we are out of work, we have to have faith the right job will come along. When we are at our wit's end with certain family relationships, we have to have faith that relationships will be restored.

God may appear to play along as a chess player in the game of life, but he controls the entire chess board. He will turn all of Satan's moves for our benefit. God made the ultimate chess move when he sent his son to die for our sins, and although he died on the cross, he rose again! Check mate! He's got us completely covered by his blood.

With faith, we can overcome anything! If God be for us, who can be against us?

Prompt 20: How is faith an armor of protection against warfare? Think of a time you have exercised tremendous faith and God proved faithful. Think of a time God strengthened your faith during a season of uncertainty.

_____

_____

_____

_____

_____

_____

_____

_____

_____

_____

_____

_____

_____

_____

_____

_____

_____

Go back to Day 1 and adjust your battle plan

There is a time for everything, and a season for every activity under the heavens:

- Ecclesiastes 3:1 (NIV)

But those who hope in the LORD
will **renew their strength**.
They will soar on wings like eagles;
they will run and not grow weary,
they will walk and not be faint.

- Isaiah 40:31 (NIV)

DAY 21

Maximize Periods of Rest

God builds in periods of rest and replenishment in the midst of the battle or after the battle. We must maximize those windows of time. Take advantage of those seasons. Get things done. Rest. Replenish your reserves. Heal. Create. Prepare. Get organized. Rest in his promises. These are opportunities to renew our strength.

There have been times in life I've had an injury or major disappointment and had a random opportunity for downtime. I wondered what God was saying during that time. Perhaps it was, "My child, stop whatever you are doing and heal. My child, I have other projects I need for you to get done. Pivot your attention. Quickly get started on another task I have for you. I have you in this place right now to learn and leave an influence, but I've also built in time for you to pursue another calling. This isn't free time. Get important things in order, refine your craft, and heal from what you have endured. Recoup from the pain. Process what you have been through. Renew your strength and set yourself up for the next battle that is closely in sight."

Rest periods can also be learning periods. This could be a time to step back, observe, and learn. God fights with us and for us. We don't have to feel we have to always be the captain, leading the force. God will show you when it's time to step back and allow others to fight, as you rest.

Be still. Nothing lasts forever. Weeping may endure for a night, but joy comes in the morning. Life is seasonal. The battle has an end date. God will deliver us from all of our hardships. Maximize seasons of rest by turning inward, reflecting, and listening for God's voice.

Prompt 21: What are you going to do to maximize your season of rest? Reflect on past resting periods. What was revealed to you during this season?

_____

_____

_____

_____

_____

_____

_____

_____

_____

_____

_____

_____

_____

_____

_____

_____

_____

Go back to Day 1 and adjust your battle plan

Though he slay me, **yet will I hope in him**; I will surely defend my ways to his face.

- Job 13:15 (NIV)

DAY 22

Remember Lessons from Job

13 Lessons from the Book of Job

#1)   We all endure challenging hardships. Right living does not ensure a life free from pain.

#2)   God may appear silent, but he's always at work on our behalf.

#3)   We may feel alone and isolated, but God is with us.

#4)   As with Job, God doesn't always explain or reveal the reason behind our suffering. There are things that only God understands. That is true faith. Trust God. Do not get fixated on knowing "the why."

#5)   There are many treasures in the trial. Difficult times stretch us and makes as grow in ways that would not be possible without the struggle. When we are tried by the fire, we come out as pure gold.

#6)   There are limits to the trial. It will NOT take us under.

#7)   Never speak against God, despite your circumstances. Don't blame God through it all.

#8)   The wait for God to show up can be agonizing, but he will show up.

#9)   Job put all his trust in God, even in hopeless circumstances. No matter what we endure, keep your hope in God.

#10)   Well intentioned friends might try to give you a rationale for your suffering. None were aware of the conversation Satan had with God.

#11)   God will restore all that we lost.

#12)   No evil comes from God.

#13)   Repent and forgive and you will be blessed. Once Job forgave and prayed for his friends, the blessings came. His prayer released the blessings.

I can relate to the last point. I had been harboring unforgiveness for many years. I was also hitting a standstill in many areas of my life. When I truly forgave in my heart, and made that clear to those toward whom I was harboring resentment, that opened up blessings for me.

Prompt 22: What can we learn about warfare by studying Job's life?

_____

_____

_____

_____

_____

_____

_____

_____

_____

_____

_____

_____

_____

_____

_____

_____

_____

_____

_____

Go back to Day 1 and adjust your battle plan

Submit yourselves, then, to God. Resist the devil, and he will flee from you.

-James 4:7 (NIV)

DAY 23

Do Good Anyway

Despite negative circumstances, continue to do good deeds. Continue to join forces with good people and make sure you fight the devil. Open doors, compliment, help, encourage. You can only overcome evil with good. Show up when no one else will. Be a support. Sacrifice when no one else will. Forgive when all signs tell you not to. Help those in an area where you are strong. Give the gift. Throw the celebration. Love the people others are unkind to. Don't turn a blind eye to wrongdoing. Be the voice. Be the one not going along with the crowd, if they are not following God's will. But don't do it for show. Most of your good deeds should be done in secret. Do good in subtle ways. Be an angel, but don't become anyone's God. Let God be God.

When people appear to not mean you well, remember it is the principality operating within that person. Time and time again I've seen people try to block blessings and intentionally cause harm, and it eventually backfires. Call it karma or the law of reaping and sowing. God vindicates. He is in control. No one gets away with continuously doing wrong and mistreating people. Despite how a person or group of people behave, do good anyway. All you say and do is kingdom work and for the glory of God.

Prompt 23: What are ways for you to do good even in the midst of the battle? How is doing good a weapon for spiritual warfare?

_____

_____

_____

_____

_____

_____

_____

_____

_____

_____

_____

_____

_____

_____

_____

_____

_____

_____

_____

Go back to Day 1 and adjust your battle plan

I press on toward the goal to win the prize for which God has called me heavenward in Christ Jesus.

- Philippians 3:14 (NIV)

DAY 24

Stay Focused

During warfare you must remain focused. Brush off the distractions and complete the assignment God is asking you to complete during this period of time. Your Godly response and temperament might be to help some of God's lost sheep to return back to him. Satan wants to catch you distracted and unprepared. The enemy will have you dwelling on the various disappointments of friends and family. He might have you worried about your job security or the attacks of criticism and incompetence. Anything to have you disconnect from God.

Dispel the discouragement. Remind yourself that Christ died for us. God gave his only begotten son for our sins. His nail-scarred hands are a testament to how he suffered so that we could be redeemed from our sins. If Christ did that for us, this present warfare will not take us under.

Don't numb out.

Don't be distracted by the strong winds.

Remain focused.

Prompt 24: What is God asking you to focus on? Why is remaining focused imperative during spiritual warfare?

_____

_____

_____

_____

_____

_____

_____

_____

_____

_____

_____

_____

_____

_____

_____

_____

_____

_____

Go back to Day 1 and adjust your battle plan

Be joyful in hope, patient in affliction, **faithful in prayer.**

- Romans 12: 12 (NIV)

DAY 25

Joy

Joy is God's presence within us. It is a choice. It's not based on people, things, or external circumstances. True joy must be present despite our situation. Don't say to yourself, "I'll be happy when the battle is over." Have peace and contentment in spite of it all. Find something to smile about despite what has happened and is happening around you. Where are the nuggets of goodness even in the midst of the storm? Be content with whatever state you are in.

As the attacks come, continue to abide in Him. Stay connected and remain with him at every moment throughout your day. He will give us His joy to radiate into this world. Reflect on God's word. Pray. Smile. Exude happiness. There should be no such thing as a sad Christian. Open your heart. Be forward thinking. Have a deep knowledge of who you belong to and who is in control. Don't allow the battle to drag you under and lose your joy. The end is near, and the lessons and blessings from the battle will abound.

There is a strong correlation between gratitude and joy. When we see the blessing in the battle, we are able to operate differently. God shows his face even in the midst of the battle. God still protects us, times things just right, meets all of our needs, and gives us something to laugh about, find comfort in, and to be in awe of. Just take a look around you. Take ownership of your joy by knowing Christ and imagining how much He loves you.

Prompt 25: In what ways are you radiating joy? What are the blessings from the most recent battle? Can you see how focusing on the storm and not on God is weighing you down and blocking the joy from your life?

_____

_____

_____

_____

_____

_____

_____

_____

_____

_____

_____

_____

_____

_____

_____

_____

_____

Go back to Day 1 and adjust your battle plan

And the peace of God, which transcends all understanding, will guard your hearts and your minds in Christ Jesus.

- Philippians 4:7 (NIV)

DAY 26

Silence to Preserve Peace

Peace is the goal. We don't have to respond to everything that comes our way. In fact, if we gave attention to everything, we would lose our sanity and become preoccupied with people and things that bear no fruit.

We also need to check on our own stress levels and levels of fatigue or trauma. If we ourselves are in a weakened state, we are not in a state to fight. There are many traps that will be set when you are not in your optimal state. This is also a time to watch your tongue. You may end up saying things that only add fuel to the warfare. We never want our words to leave a lasting imprint.

At the peak of the warfare, lean into those who bring you peace. Step back from those who tend to bring about frustration and agitation. You must exercise discernment. Is this worth a response? Be still. Don't throw stones at every dog that barks.

Prompt 26: How is silence a weapon against warfare? Recall a time when demonic forces attempted to stir you up. Was silence used as a response? If so, how was that beneficial? Do you regret a time you retaliated with words when you should have used silence?

_____

_____

_____

_____

_____

_____

_____

_____

_____

_____

_____

_____

_____

_____

_____

_____

_____

_____

_____

Go back to Day 1 and adjust your battle plan

For though we live in the world, we do not wage war as the world does. The weapons we fight with are not the weapons of the world. On the contrary, **they have divine power to demolish strongholds.** We demolish arguments and every pretension that sets itself up against the knowledge of God, and we take captive every thought to make it obedient to Christ.

- 2 Corinthians 10:3-5 (NIV)

DAY 27

Apply Lessons from The Art of War

The Art of War by Chinese strategist Sun Tzu delves into warfare and military strategy. It is a book worth reading. We can apply some of those same principles to spiritual warfare.

#1)   Speak up only when necessary.

#2)   Choose your battles. Fight only when there is something to be gained. The best fight is to not fight at all. Is it worth it? Some you cannot win. Some you can win, but at too high a cost. Everyone suffers from prolonged warfare.

#3)   Know your enemy and know yourself.

#4)   Emotions are short-lived. Keep them in check. Your actions have consequences.

#5)   Don't let your ego lead you.

#6)   Keep switching up your strategy.

#7)   Don't be intimidated by chaos.

#8)   Get rid of the stray sheep that disrupt your fight.

#9)   War is all about deception. Appear weak even when strong. "They" are always watching, to catch you sleeping.

#10) Timing is very important. Think through key moves that you make.

Prompt 27: What is the connection between *The Art of War* and spiritual warfare? Reread the lessons above. Which one resonates with you the most?

_____

_____

_____

_____

_____

_____

_____

_____

_____

_____

_____

_____

_____

_____

_____

_____

_____

Go back to Day 1 and adjust your battle plan

"For I know the plans I have for you," declares the Lord, "**plans to prosper you** and not to harm you, **plans to give you hope and a future**."

- Jeremiah 29:11 (NIV)

DAY 28

Purpose

The enemy will attack your strengths and gifts. That is a threat to him. No matter the attacks, remember God has gifted you in a certain way for a reason. He wants you to use your gifts to glorify his name. The battle will be most prominent in your area of gifting. Roll up your sleeves and get into it.

The purpose of your position is to bless God's people with your gifts. Similar to gratitude, when we focus less on the battle itself and focus on what's greater, such as what God has ordained for our lives, the battle holds less power in our lives.

God has specific battles he only wants you to fight. He has already mapped out your strategic positioning. We must focus on God's purpose for our lives.

Prompt 28: What is your purpose? How has the enemy waged a war in this area of your life? How does knowing your area of giftedness and that it will be attacked set you up for warfare?

_____

_____

_____

_____

_____

_____

_____

_____

_____

_____

_____

_____

_____

_____

_____

_____

Go back to Day 1 and adjust your battle plan

"...**No weapon forged against you will prevail**,
and you will refute every tongue that accuses you.
This is the heritage of the servants of the LORD,
and this is their vindication from me,"
declares the LORD.

- Isaiah 54:17 (NIV)

DAY 29

Employ Daily Battle Strategies

#1)   Remember who you are in Christ.

#2)   Don't give up or give in. When you are at your wit's end with a situation you know God proclaimed for you, hang on. It's always too soon to quit.

#3)   Rebuke the enemy and cast him away, out loud: "Satan, flee!"

#4)   Smile and create happy moments.

#5)   Remember: God is the only source of completion. It isn't the likes on social media, alcohol, the opposite sex, job titles, etc.

#6)   Pick and choose your battles.

#7)   Ignore. Brush it off. Keep a smile on your face.

#8)   Ask clarifying questions.

#9)   Take a restoration break.

#10) Blinders on – accomplish the original goal.

#11) Focus on the positive: How has the universe conspired on your behalf recently?

#12) Pivot your attention to something else that needs your attention.

#13) Create.

#14) Contribute.

#15) Embody someone you admire, like Michelle Obama: "When they go low, you go high."

#16) Remember the Four Agreements, by Don Miguel Ruiz:
    A) Be impeccable with your words;
    B) Don't take anything personally;

C) Don't make assumptions;

D) Always do your best.

#17) Before you speak, ask yourself, Is it kind? Is it true? Is it necessary? Does it improve upon the silence?

#18) Do not focus on other people's deficiencies.

#19) Remember: God makes certain requests of you to stretch you.

#20) Encourage and validate others.

#21) Take time to rest and recuperate alone.

#22) Have a visual reminder of the people and things that inspire you as well as your goals.

#23) Continue to use the strength of your voice not to accept things that aren't right.

#24) Look out for the light of God in the midst of the darkness. This appears as little angel messengers that bring you comfort.

#25) Remove evil people and things from your home.

#26) Learn as much as you can in the place you're currently in.

#27) Ask God each day to assign you the angel that will take charge over you and your family.

Prompt 29: What every day strategies resonate with you the most? Why is having a daily battle plan with specific strategies vital as a weapon of warfare?

_____

_____

_____

_____

_____

_____

_____

_____

_____

_____

_____

_____

_____

_____

_____

_____

Go back to Day 1 and adjust your battle plan

Finally, my brethren, be strong in the Lord, and in the power of His might. **Put on the whole armor of God,** that ye may be able to stand against the wiles of the devil.

- Ephesians 6:10-11 (NIV)

DAY 30

Be Strong in the Lord. Endure.

People are betting on you to quit and be defeated. Endure. Don't fall for it. We as believers know God's track record. There is a blessing on the other side of the battle. Be a witness. You are representing Christ.

Continuously seek him. Continuously pray, praise his name, and use the armor we have discussed for the past 29 days. Combine with other believers and fight when there is something to be gained. Don't continue to waste your time, energy, and resources on low-level demons. Continue to enter places and spaces that are loving and value you; where they roll out the red carpet and see you as a blessing. Continue to enter the spaces that aren't as welcoming, but where God has assigned you to be.

There have been moments I've been so tired of fighting. The enemy wants you exhausted so that you stop pushing. You stop trying. So that you give up. At times like these, pray for supernatural strength. Your final push could be a matter of life or death. What if the Israelites gave up before reaching the promise land? Or Job gave up before everything was restored? I want you to remember though that it is GOD who fights for us. If you are beyond exhausted, something is wrong. Our human capabilities are limited.

Don't be distracted by the strong wind or the forces around you that are working against you. Pick yourself up, brush yourself off, and continue to fight the good fight. The sting of the attacks can feel overwhelming and extremely painful. Strategize. Keep your eyes fixed on God, who is in complete control. Consider his track record and all of your past victories. REMAIN FOCUSED. Don't give up.

God is strengthening us. He is preparing us. God cleans things up, cuts things into shape, streamlines particular areas, so his work can be done. God prunes you from one situation to prepare you for something greater. This battle is a painful season of preparation, but God is ALWAYS with you.

As was stated in the beginning, the enemy has already been defeated. The battle has already been won. We know the end of this story. Just be strong and steadfast. Armor up in scripture, prayer, and praise. Weather the storm. Be battle ready, armored up in Christ!

Prompt 30: How does being strong in the Lord serve as a weapon for warfare? Reflect on the past 30 days. How have you shifted in terms of your perspective on warfare?

_____

_____

_____

_____

_____

_____

_____

_____

_____

_____

_____

_____

_____

_____

_____

_____

_____

Go back to Day 1 and adjust your battle plan

CONCLUSION

The following are some concluding points:

1. What are the blessings and lessons in this season of warfare? Maybe I refine my focus. Maybe I start paying attention to that child who is crying out for help. Maybe I refocus on my health.
2. Don't respond when wound up and overwhelmed. Always wait to reset. Never act out of a state of pain and confusion. Don't leave a lasting impact with a reaction to a temporary situation.
3. Be still and know who is God. Hold tight and get through, day by day. I can't emphasize this enough: Stay focused.
4. Put on the full armor of God every day.
5. Say little and give things time. There is no need to retaliate or seek payback. If someone attacks you, let God handle them. Do not judge. When others try to discredit you, they eventually end up discrediting themselves.
6. Be disciplined to withstand the tricks. He creeps in, in unexpected ways. Don't walk right into the trap the enemy sets for you.
7. The enemy will hit you in your areas of greatest strength, greatest weakness, and of greatest influence.
8. Most satanic activity is a distraction, set up to cause division.
9. Withstand temptation with the eyes or using anything as a crutch (dependency). Turn away.
10. Things tend to snowball. A little sin can quickly become a big sin.

11. The crisis may be a wake-up call or a chance to redirect our attention to other things that need our attention.
12. Tribulation draws us back to God. It allows our faith to grow. Stay close to Him at all times. Focus on God.
13. Follow the prompting of the Holy Spirit and be obedient. Pay attention and keep your eyes open.
14. Don't give up on God just because you have bad experiences.
15. Be alert to the angels God sends into your life in human form.
16. Don't let anything of importance go unmanned.
17. Only fight the high-level battles, ignore the small ones. Ask God for direction prior to fighting any battle.
18. There are times you have to be meek, humble, and submissive, and God will turn the tables for your benefit.
19. Reconcile sooner than later...a hug, a walk, a text.
20. Don't be distracted by becoming overly busy. We often want so badly to remain in the fold, on the frontlines of what's happening, but we can fall into the trap of mistaking being busy for being productive and bearing fruit. Ask God for guidance.
21. Giving also refers to your time and talent. What seeds are you sowing? God gave you certain gifts he wants you to use for his glory. Follow the prompting of the Holy Spirit to know when to step up and offer yourself up as a blessing to others.
22. We must remember that we have authority over demons. You have to fight for your life and not let the enemy stop you from pursuing your calling and highest aspirations in life. Remain firm, consistent, steadfast, and rooted in his love.
23. Build yourself up to a place of strength so that words can't easily penetrate you.
24. Don't forget who you are in Christ.

Read the following passage:

I am a tree

I am a tree
With strong roots that stem to various lands I am yet to discover.
In fact, we are all trees
Rooted in knowing we are wonderfully made on purpose with a purpose

Roots are important...they keep us grounded...especially during life's battles
Warfare simply serves as a refinement to an already strong firm and bountiful tree

The storms may rock
I may lose a few leaves in the process
But my roots remain firm...

I rise with new strength…
Stronger
Wiser
Bolder
More compassionate
More empathetic

I might stand alone in a meadow, fighting the battle as one...
Or a pine tree in a forest among several trees
Being lovingly assimilated and taken into the fold
But no matter where I stand,
I have to remember who I am
and whose I am

So, go through the winter
Go through the storm
Address the leaks in your roots...
Allow growth to take place...

Ever evolving,
Ever growing...
Resting in the safety of His arms...
Always protected
Despite my weaknesses
Despite the weight of the attacks

I must manage my resistance to the storms...
Lean into my faith...
Armor up for battle...
While cutting myself and others some slack
For doing the best we can on the battle line...
Solid, firm, and rooted
Remembering always,
I am a tree

ABOUT THE AUTHOR

Sheryl Walker is an educator and has facilitated 100+ one-on-one adult coaching conversations. Her writing is inspired by her own life journey and those she has coached professionally. Her books are centered around personal growth through the acquisition of new learning, self-reflection, and daily writing. Daily writing has often served as an enlightenment ritual for her personally as a way to endure life's most challenging moments. She is also the author of the books *More Grateful: A 21-day writing journey to increase gratitude*, *Waiting Well: A 21-Day Writing Journey to Increase Patience*, *Forgive Anyway: A 30-day Writing Journey to Total Forgiveness*, and *Love Poems to God*. She enjoys writing in her leisure.